SONGS FROM CHILDHOOD
FOR EASY CLASSICAL PIANO

— PIANO LEVEL —
INTERMEDIATE

ISBN 978-1-4950-9378-4

7777 W. BLUEMOUND RD. P.O. BOX 13819 MILWAUKEE, WI 53213

In Australia Contact:
Hal Leonard Australia Pty. Ltd.
4 Lentara Court
Cheltenham, Victoria, 3192 Australia
Email: ausadmin@halleonard.com.au

Visit Hal Leonard Online at
www.halleonard.com

Visit Phillip at
www.phillipkeveren.com

PREFACE

This collection features melodies that have lit up the lives of children around the world for generations. These simple, straightforward melodies lend themselves beautifully to classical compositional devices, and the character piano pieces that emerge here are the result of this natural pairing.

This book is dedicated to Charlie John Keveren, our first grandchild, who blessed us with his arrival in 2016.

Musically yours,

Phillip Keveren

BIOGRAPHY

Phillip Keveren, a multi-talented keyboard artist and composer, has composed original works in a variety of genres from piano solo to symphonic orchestra. Mr. Keveren gives frequent concerts and workshops for teachers and their students in the United States, Canada, Europe, and Asia. Mr. Keveren holds a B.M. in composition from California State University Northridge and a M.M. in composition from the University of Southern California.

CONTENTS

ALOUETTE

Traditional
Arranged by Phillip Keveren

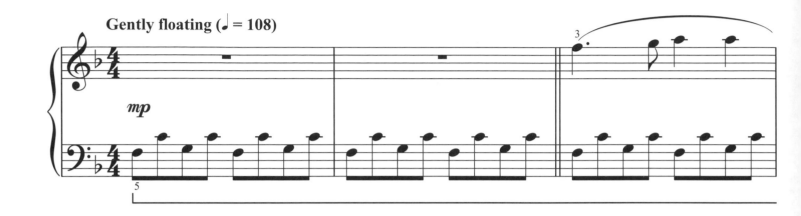

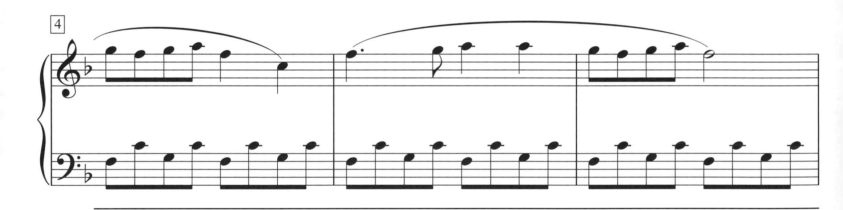

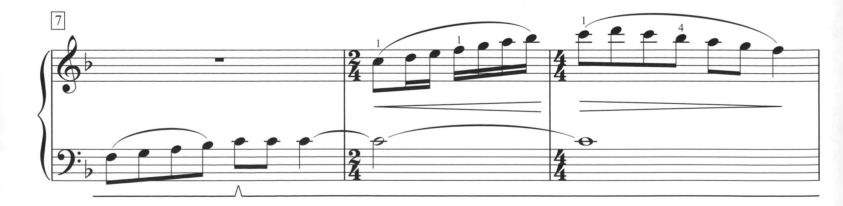

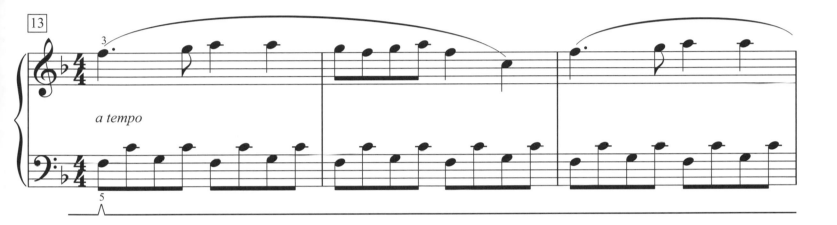

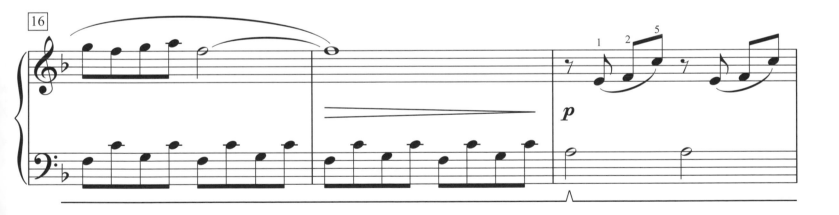

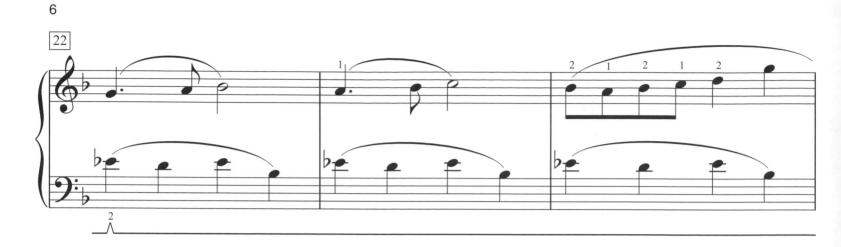

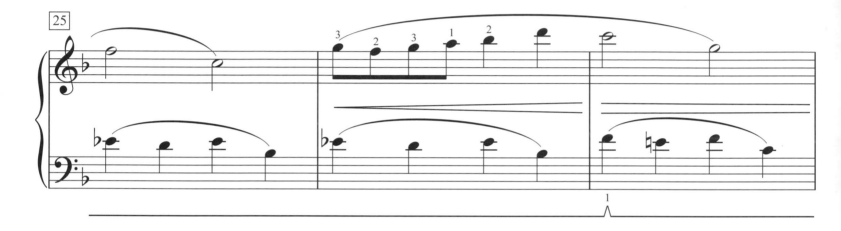

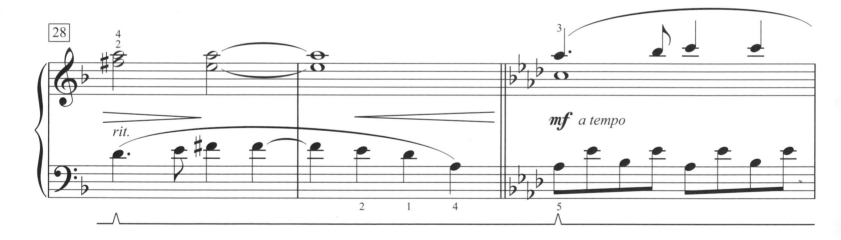

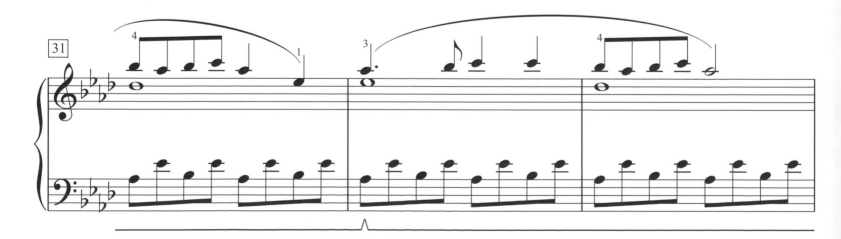

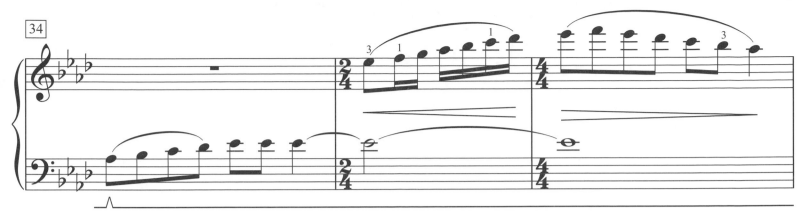

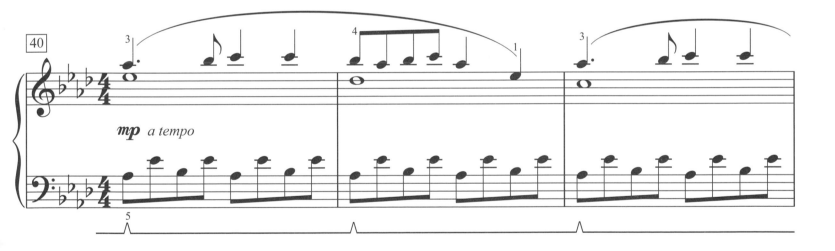

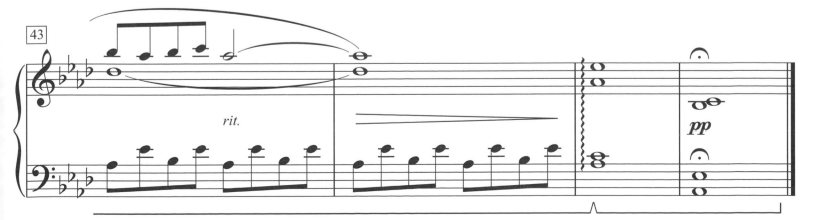

THE BEAR WENT OVER THE MOUNTAIN

Traditional
Arranged by Phillip Keveren

Lumbering (♩. = 80)

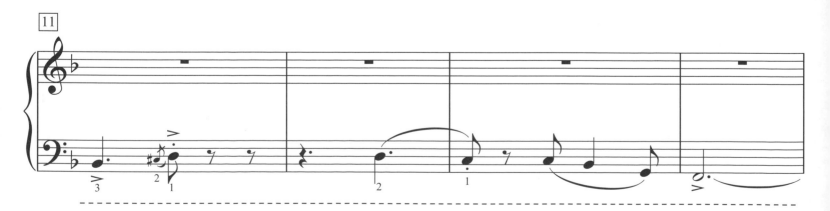

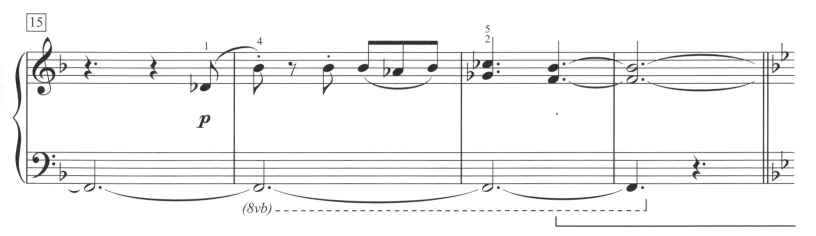

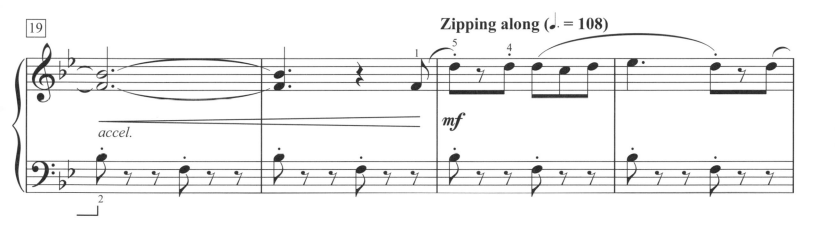

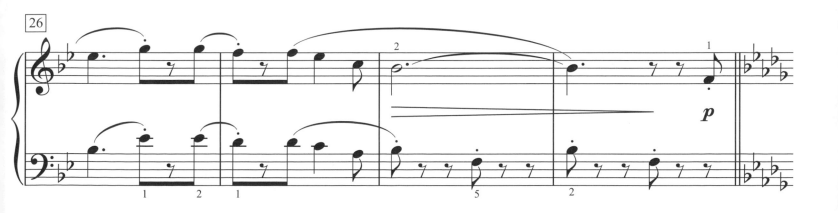

Almost out of control (♩. = 116)

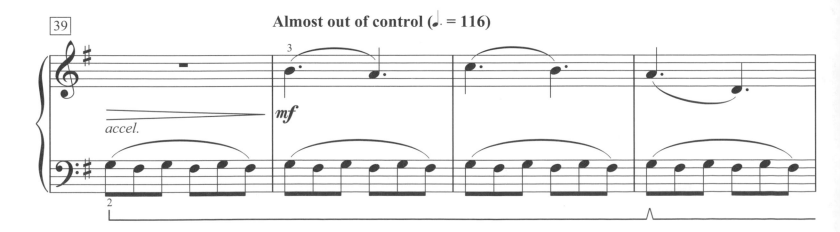

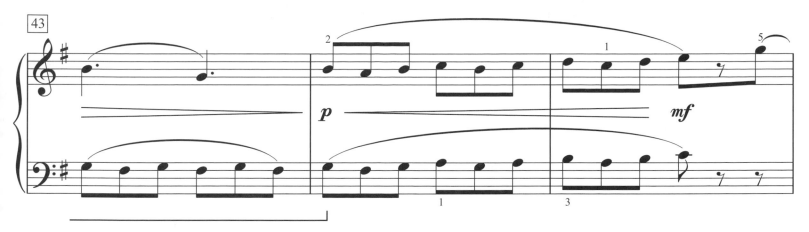

Suddenly slower (♩. = 92)
R.H. over L.H.

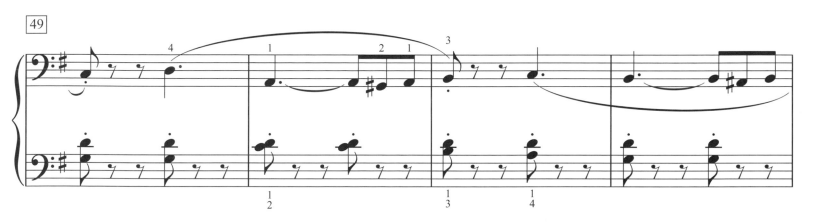

Lickety-split (♩. = 120)

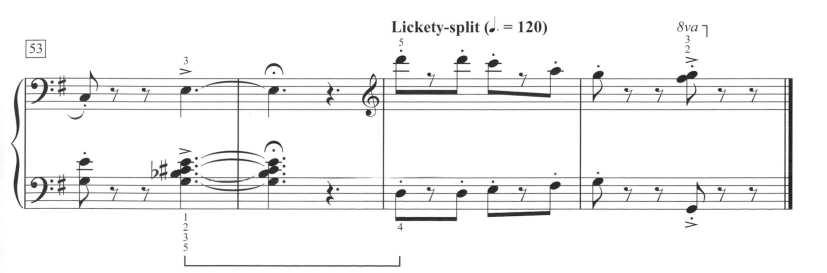

EENCY WEENSY SPIDER

Traditional
Arranged by Phillip Keveren

Steady (♩. = 104)

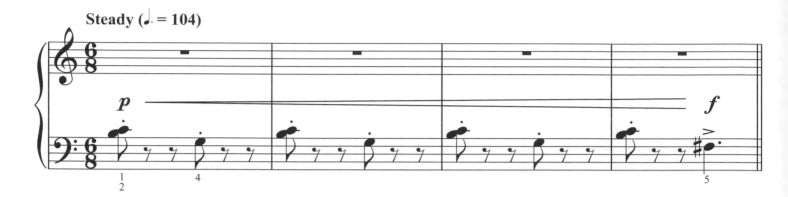

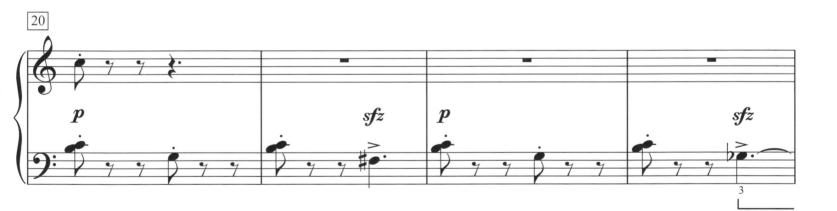

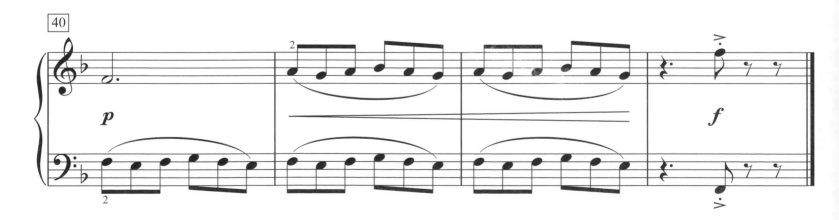

GRANDFATHER'S CLOCK

By HENRY CLAY WORK
Arranged by Phillip Keveren

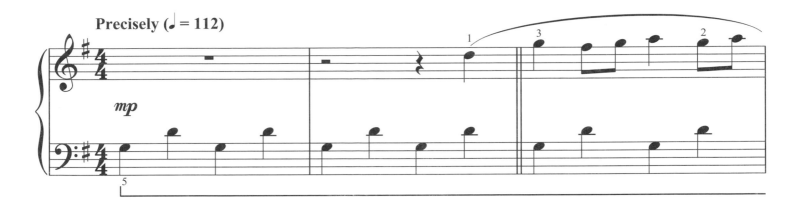

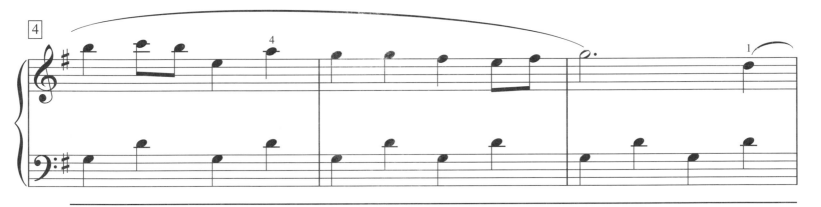

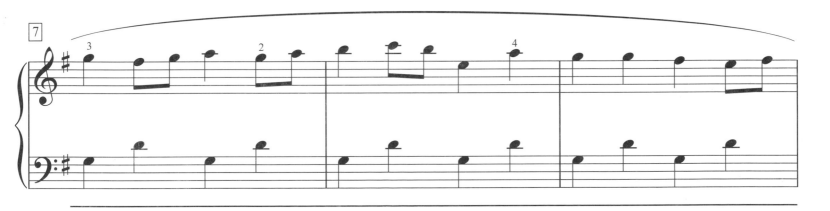

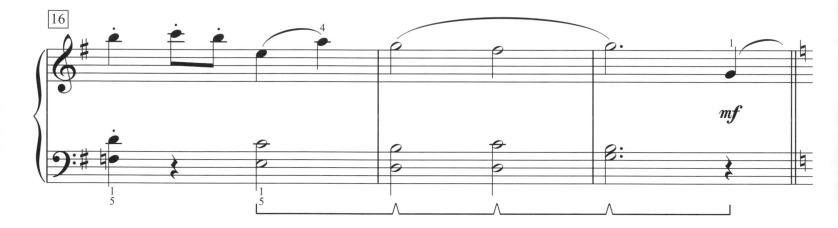

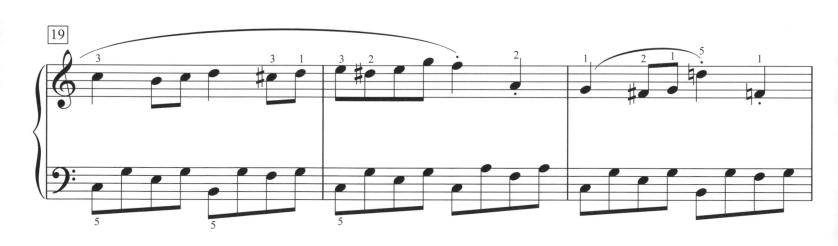

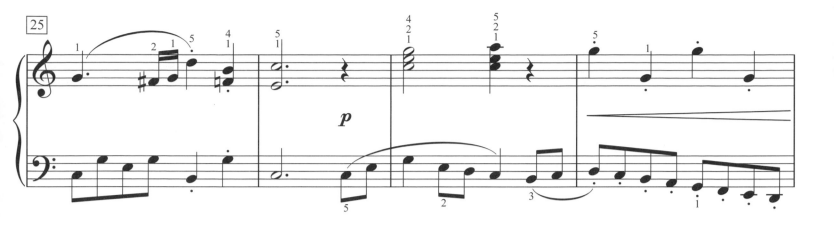

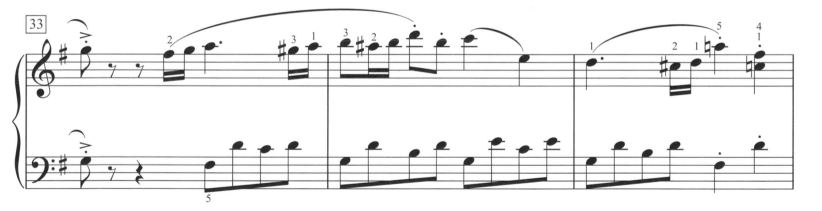

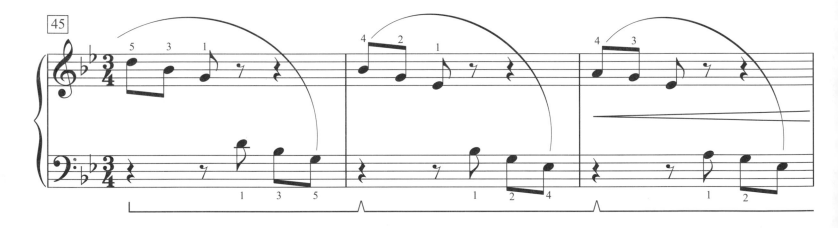

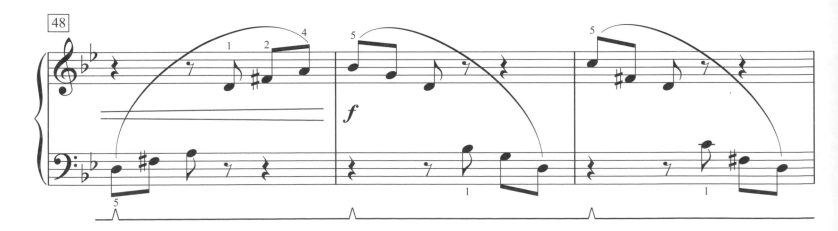

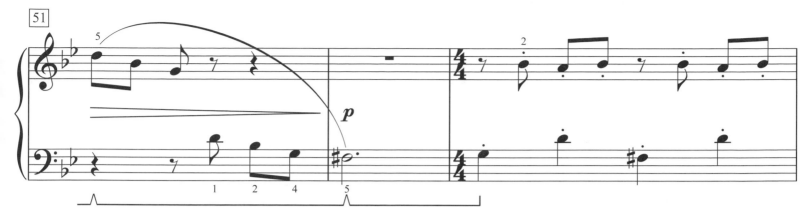

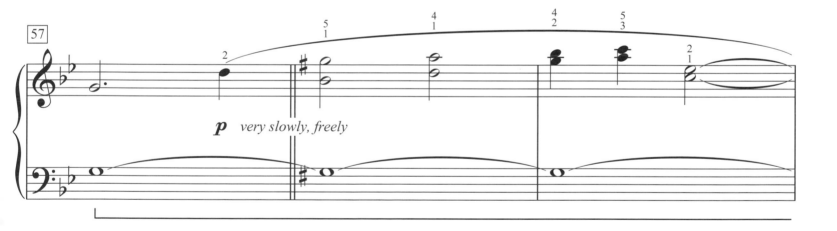

HICKORY DICKORY DOCK

Traditional
Arranged by Phillip Keveren

Persistently (♩. = 84)

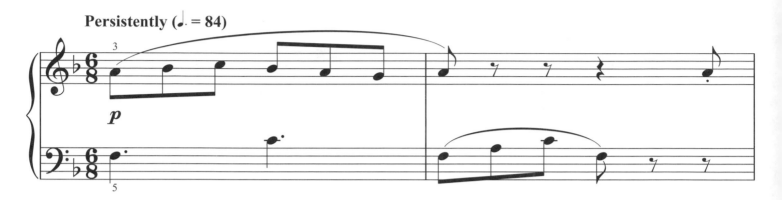

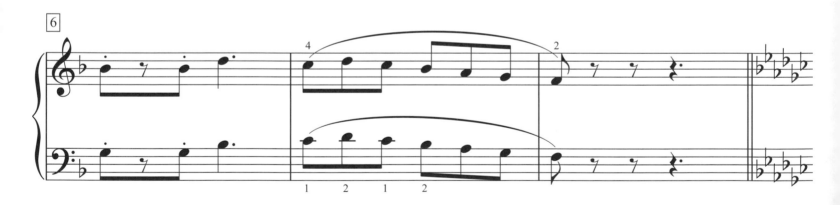

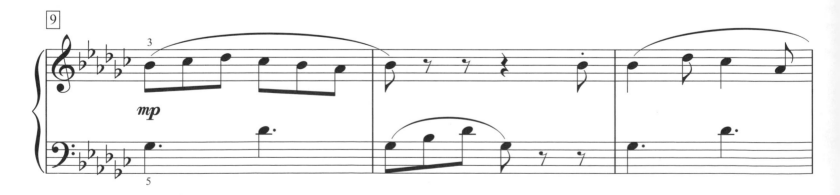

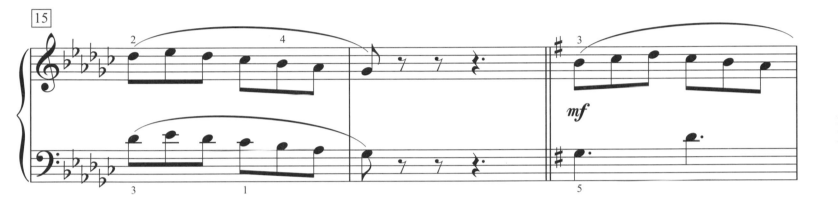

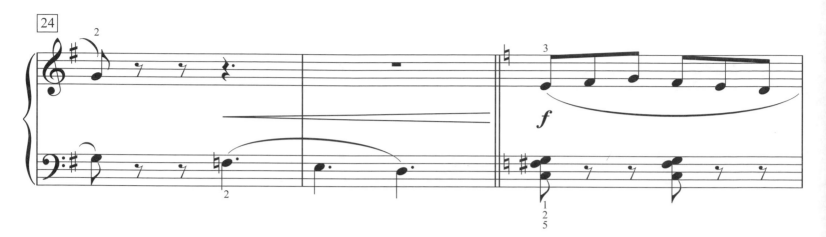

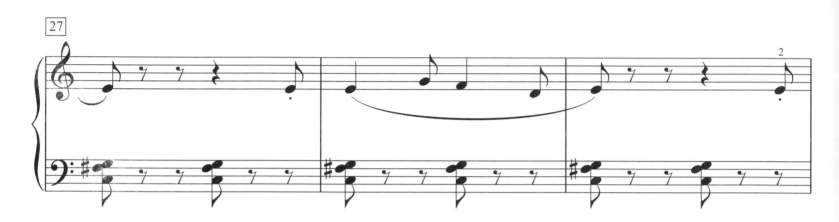

HUSH, LITTLE BABY

Carolina Folk Lullaby
Arranged by Phillip Keveren

Like a music box (♩ = 100)

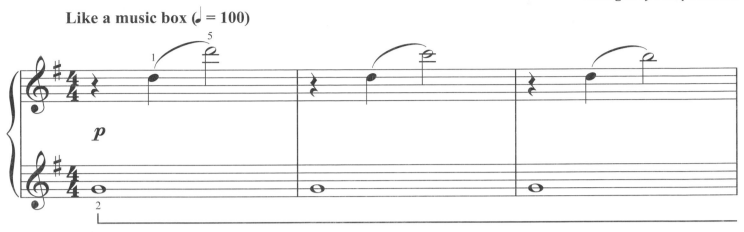

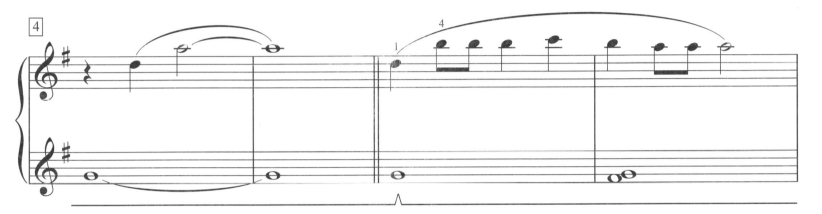

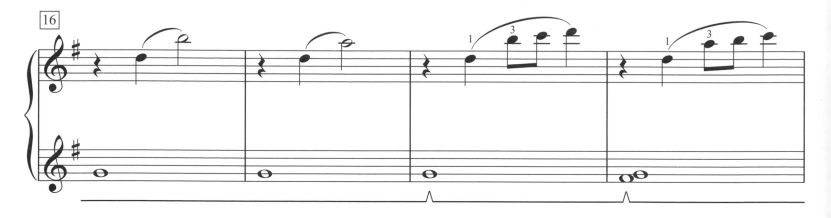

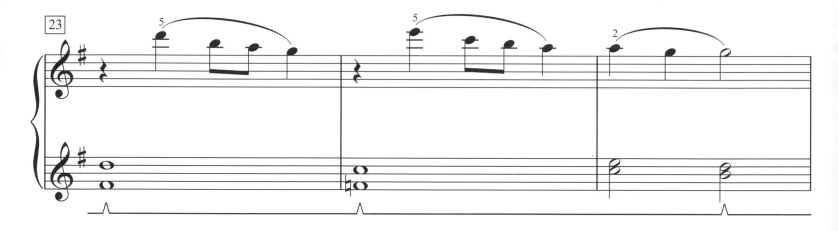

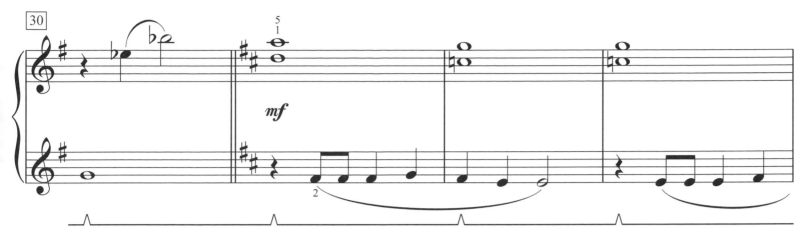

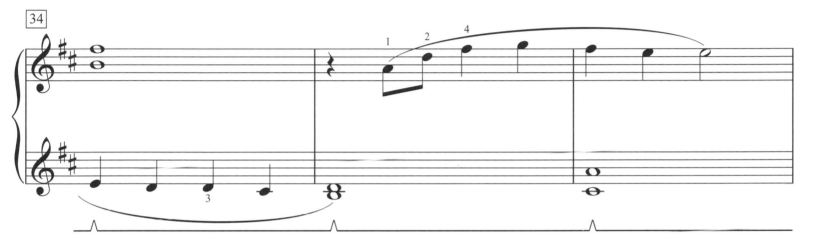

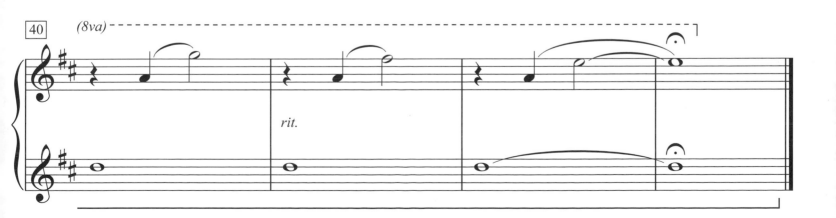

IT'S RAINING, IT'S POURING

Traditional
Arranged by Phillip Keveren

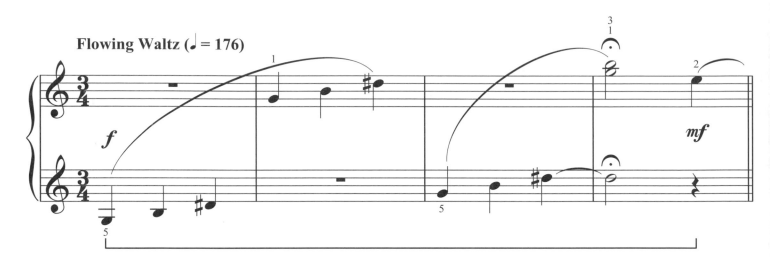

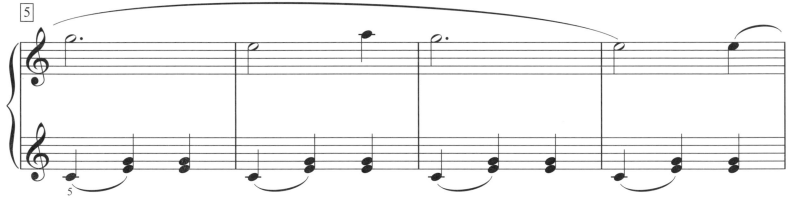

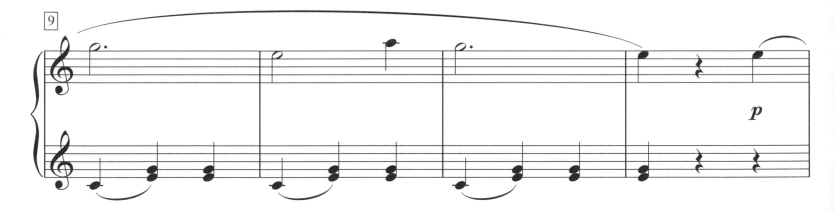

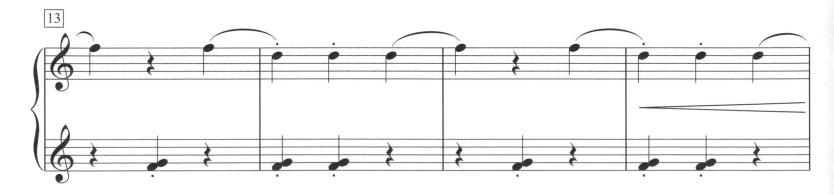

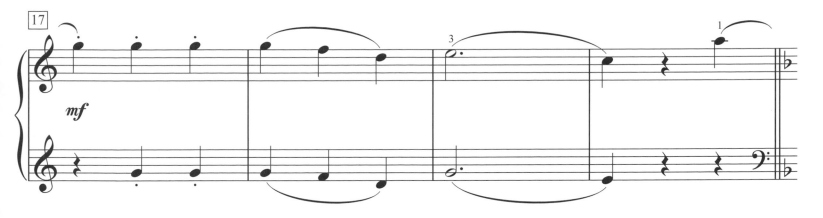

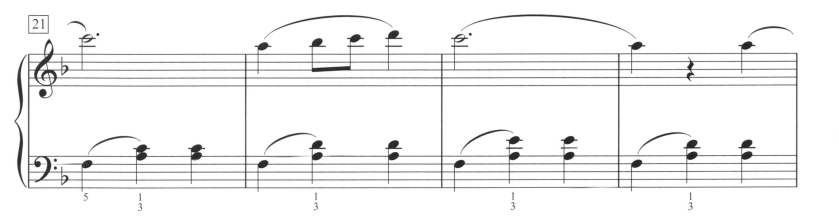

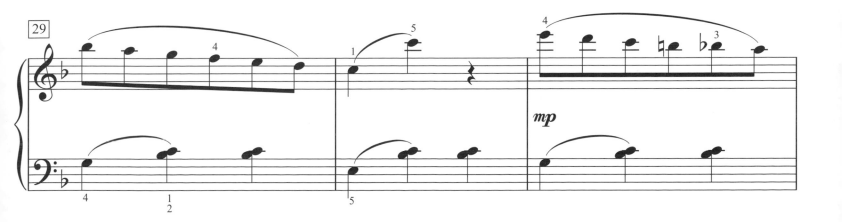

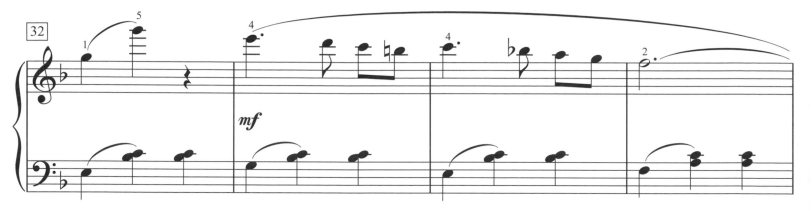

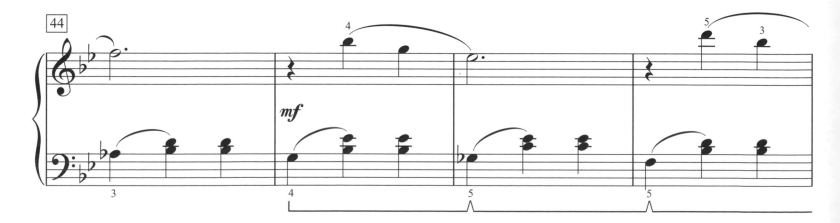

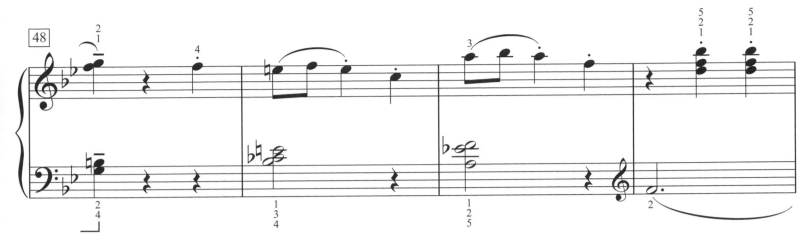

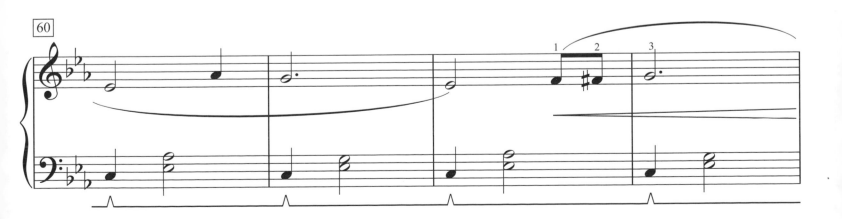

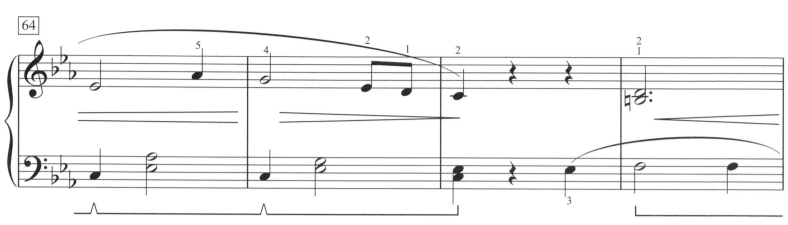

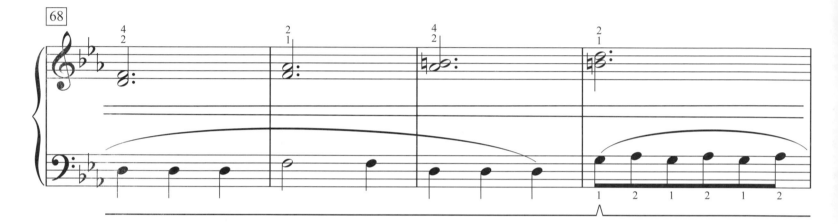

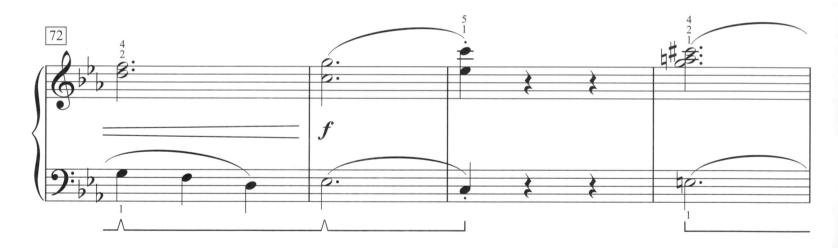

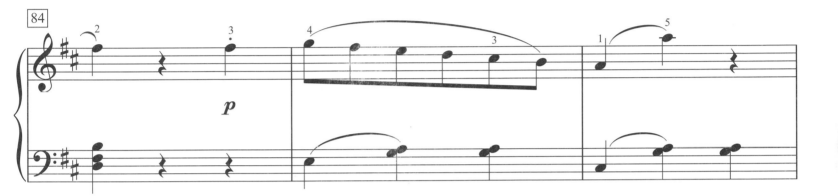

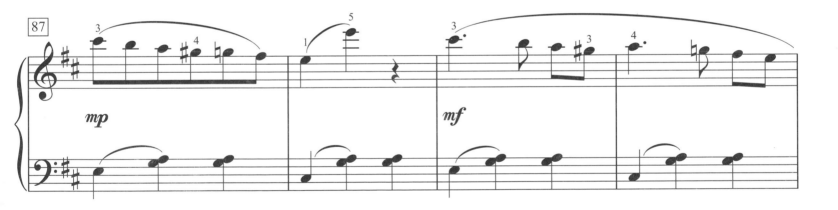

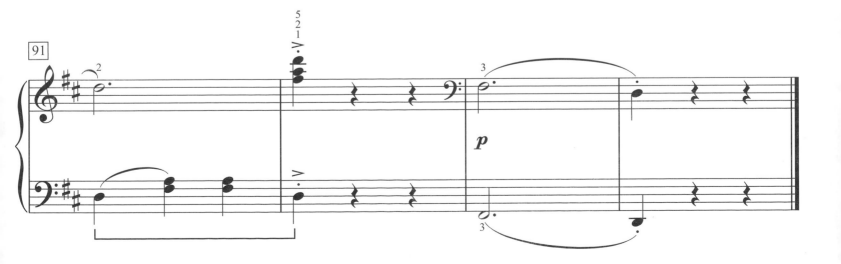

LONDON BRIDGE

Traditional
Arranged by Phillip Keveren

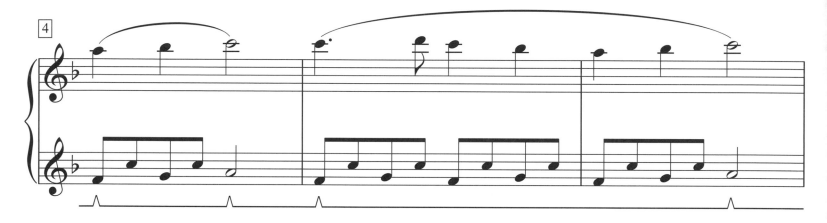

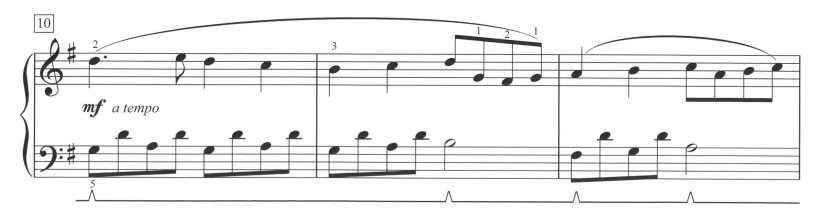

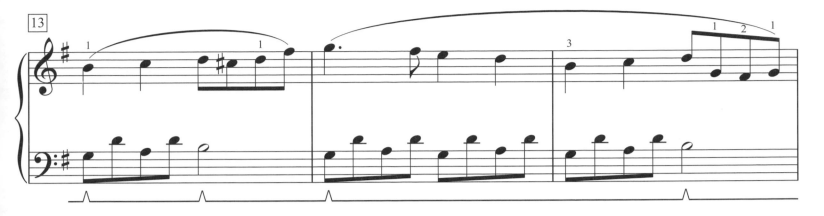

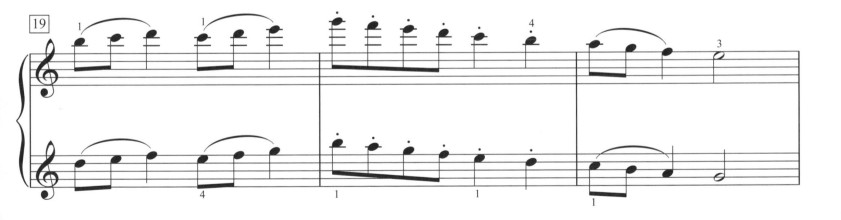

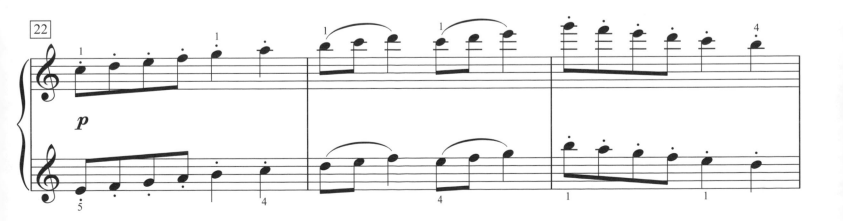

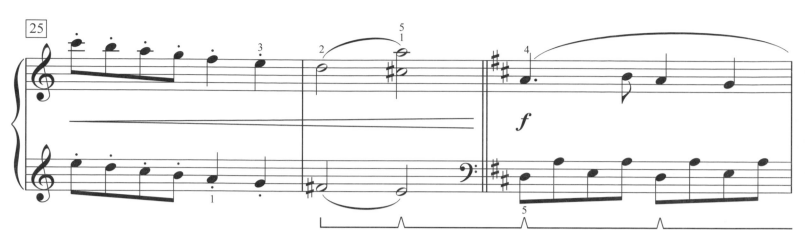

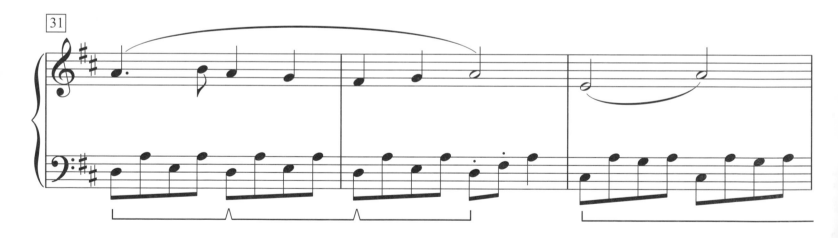

OH WHERE, OH WHERE HAS MY LITTLE DOG GONE

Words by SEP. WINNER
Traditional
Arranged by Phillip Keveren

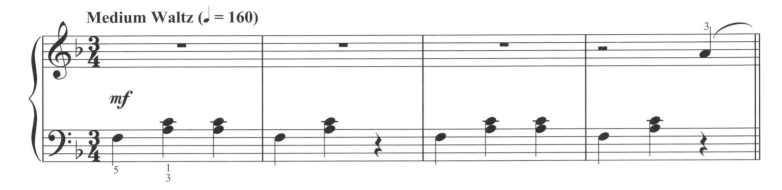

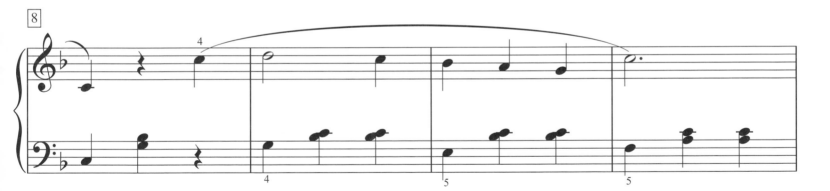

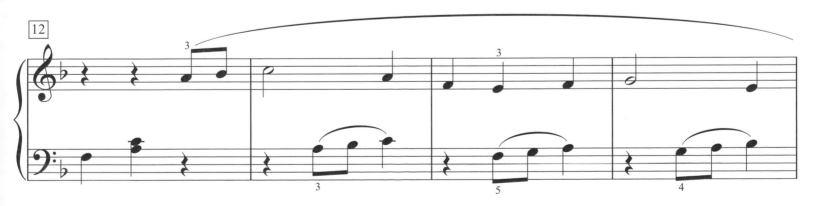

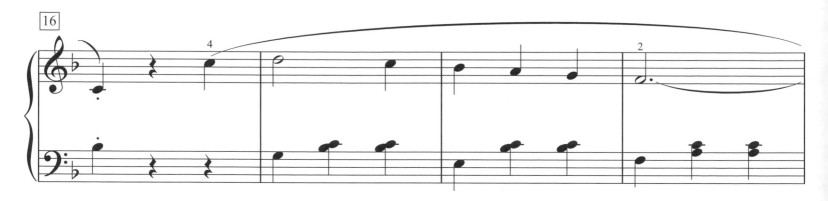

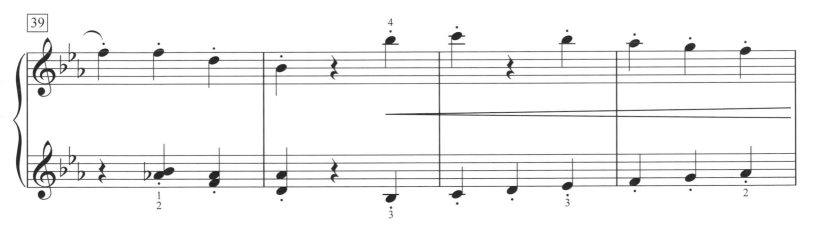

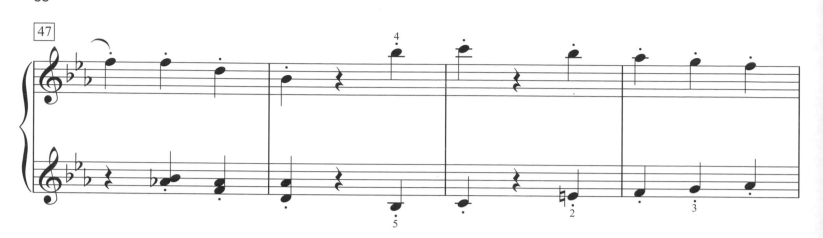

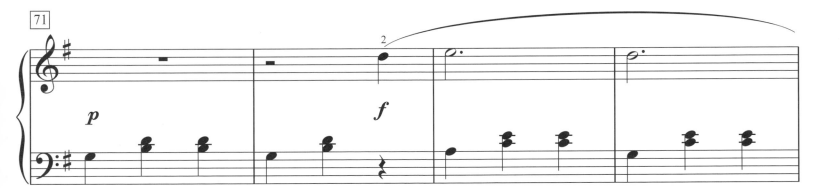

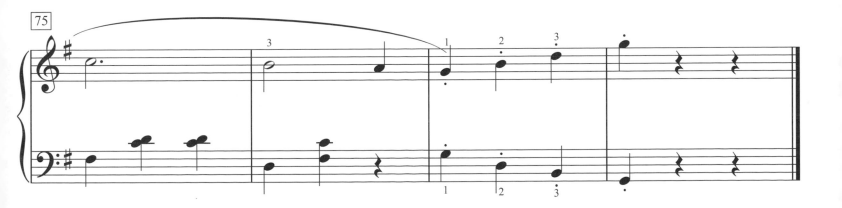

THE MUFFIN MAN

Traditional
Arranged by Phillip Keveren

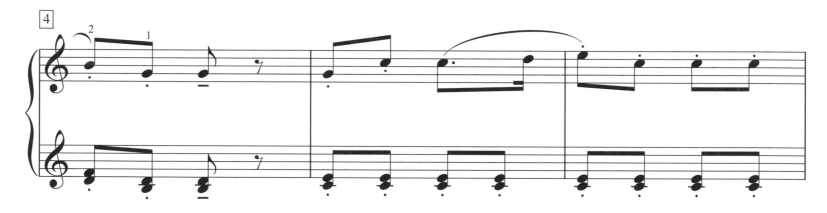

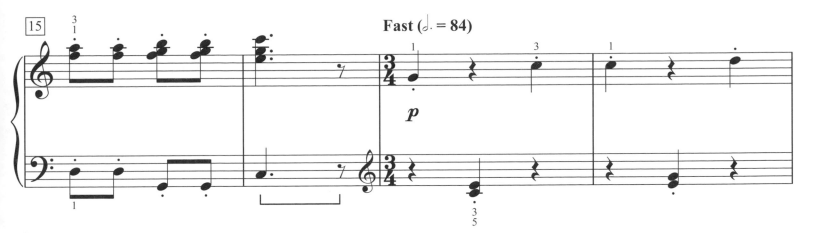

Fast (♩. = 84)

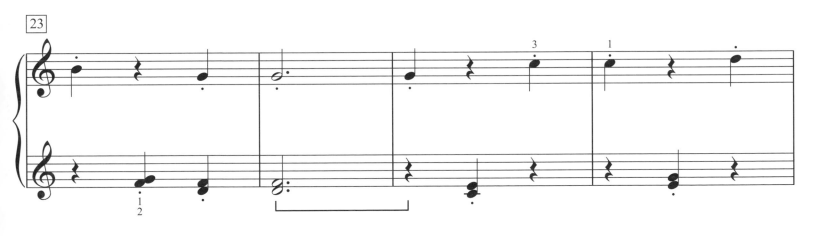

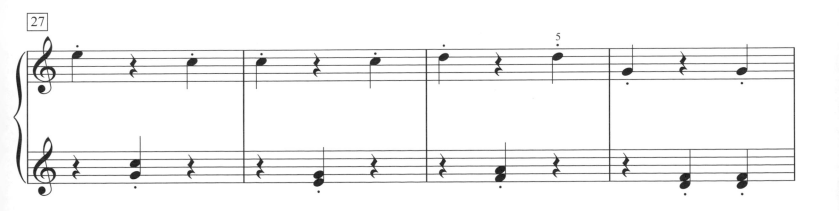

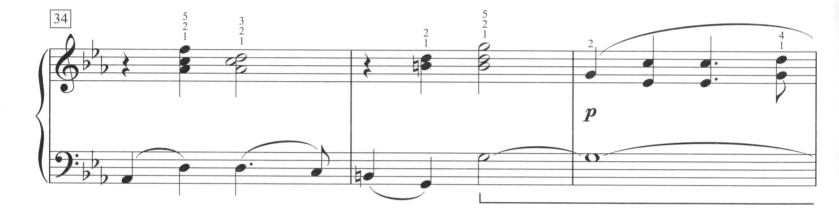

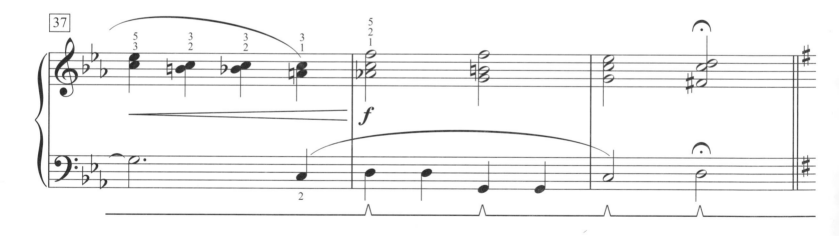

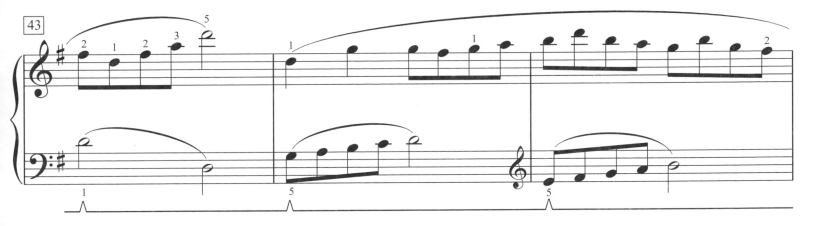

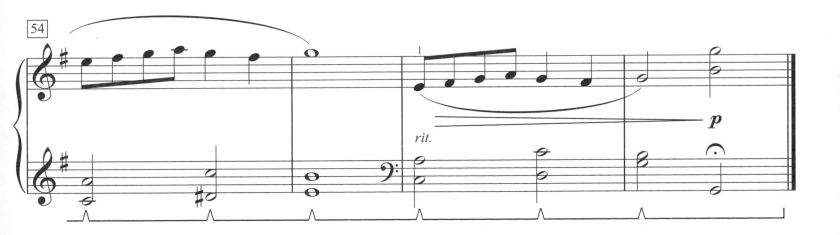

MY BONNIE LIES OVER THE OCEAN

Traditional
Arranged by Phillip Keveren

Buoyant (♩ = 160)

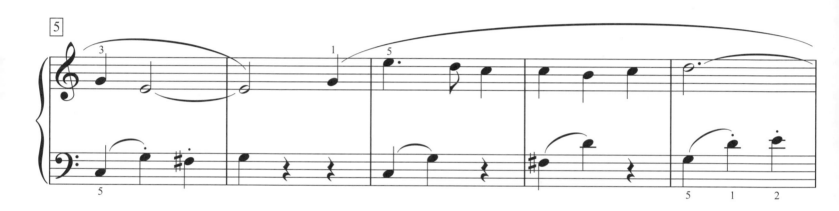

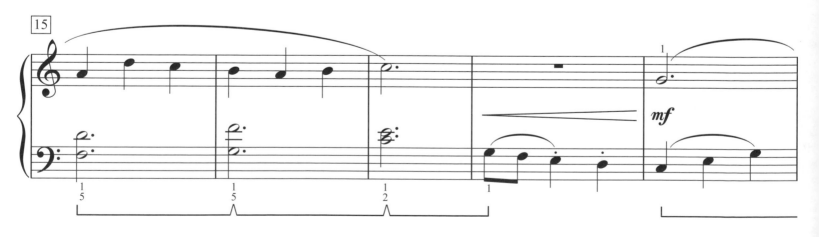

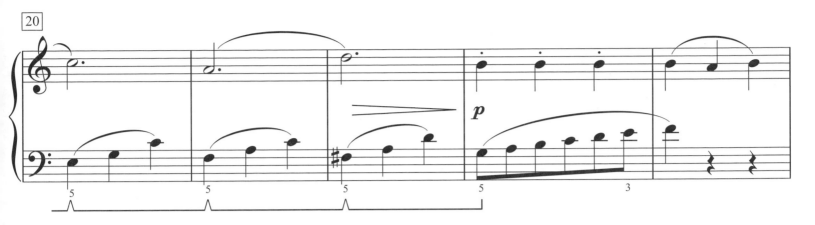

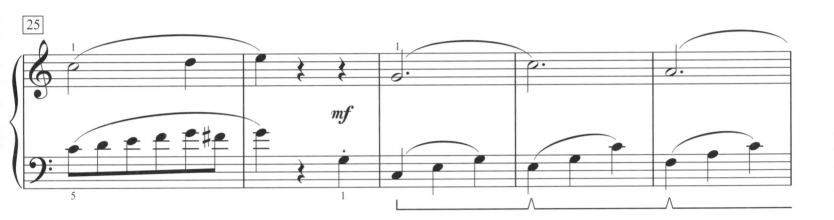

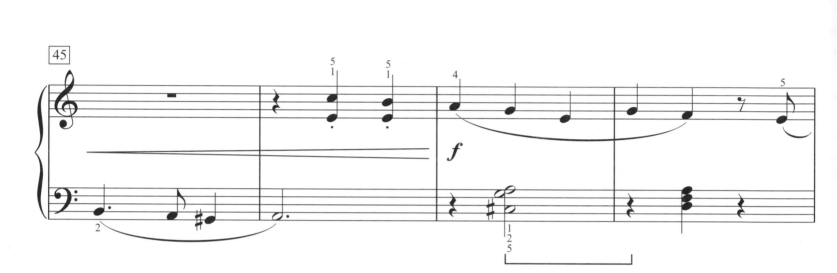

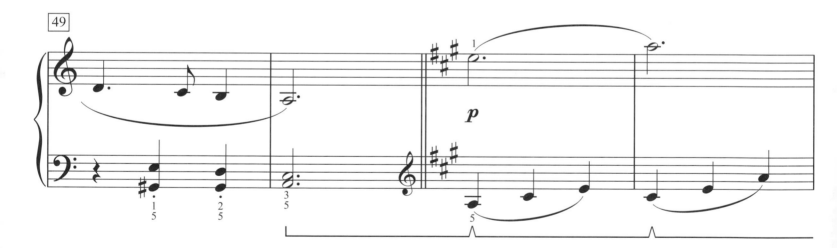

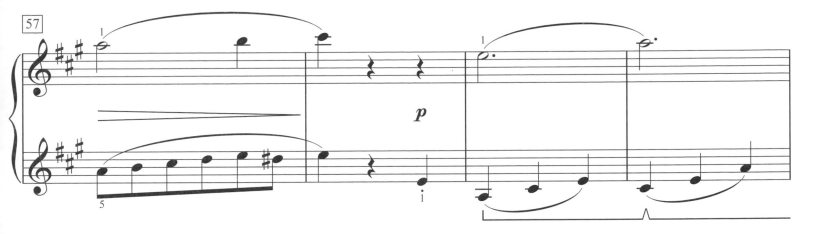

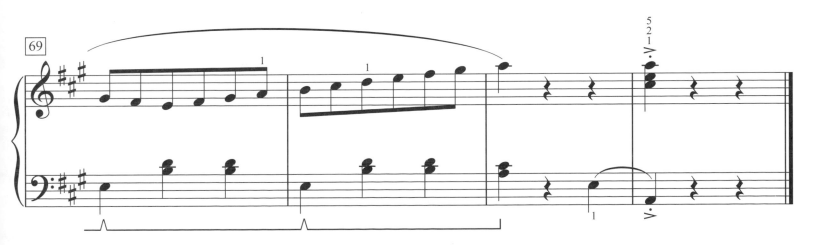

POP GOES THE WEASEL

Traditional
Arranged by Phillip Keveren

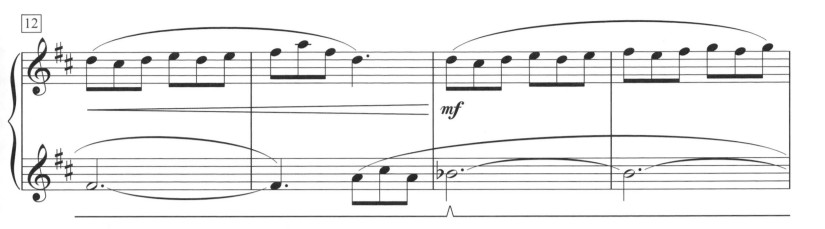

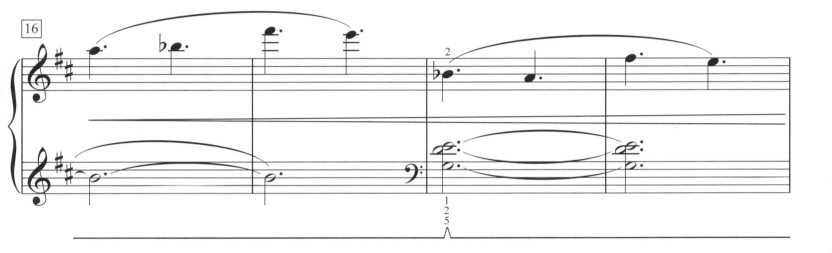

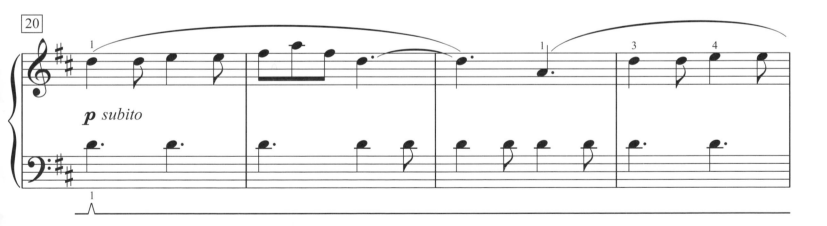

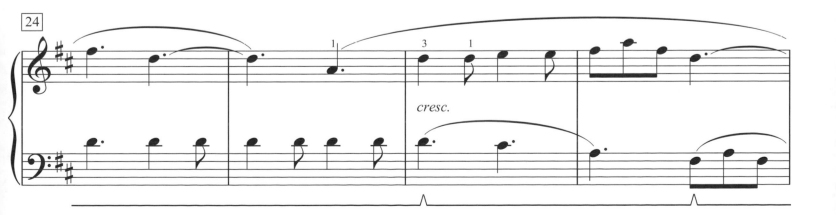

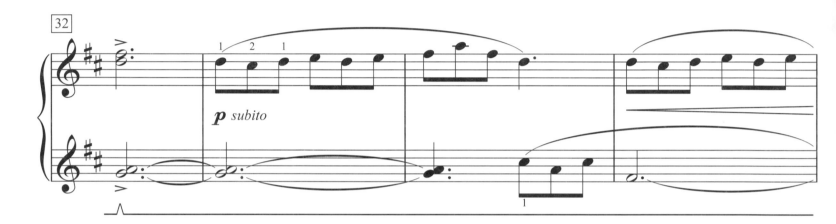

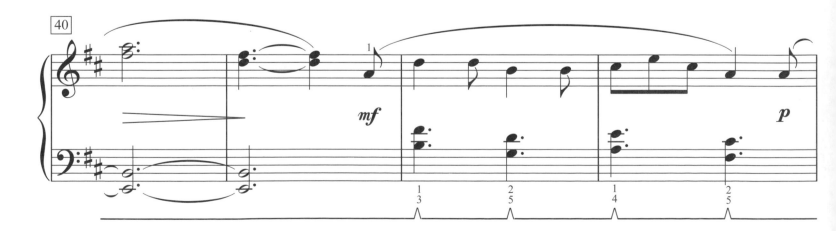

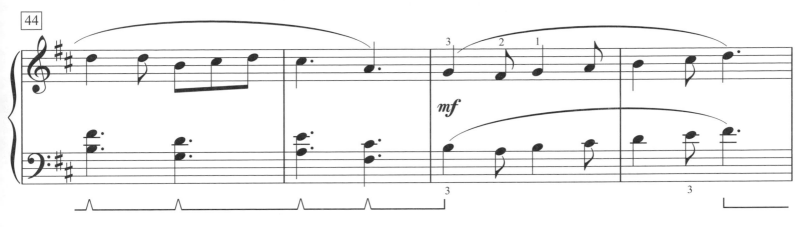

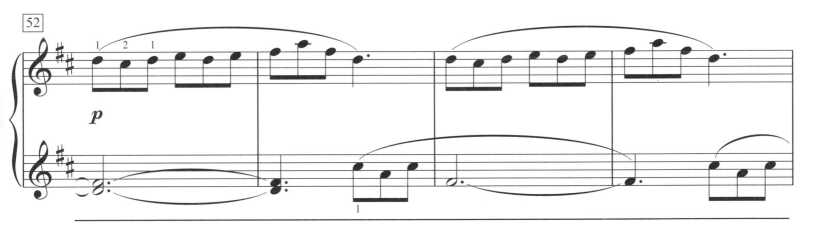

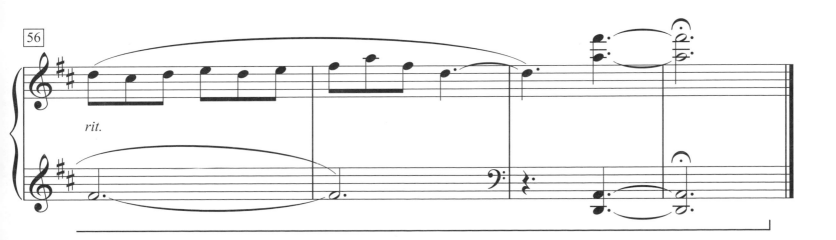

THREE BLIND MICE

Traditional
Arranged by Phillip Keveren

Scampering (♩ = 108)

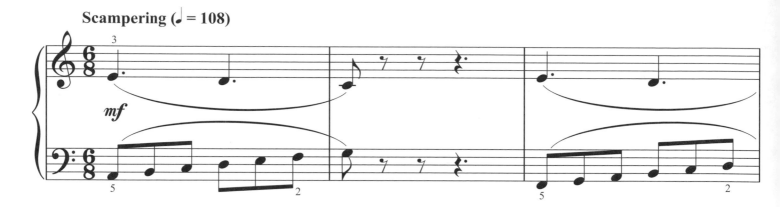

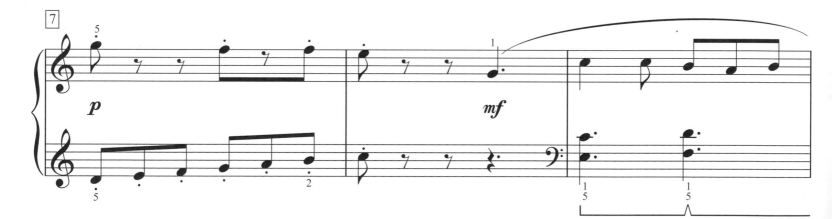

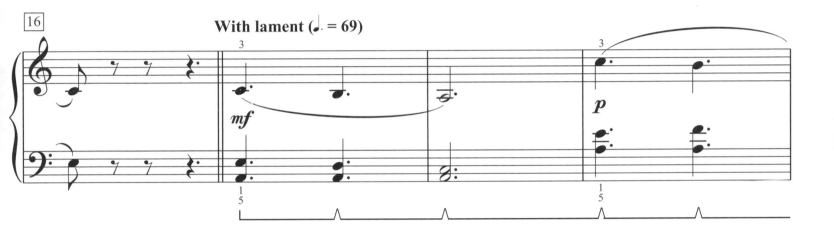

With lament (♩. = 69)

Tempo I (♩. = 108)

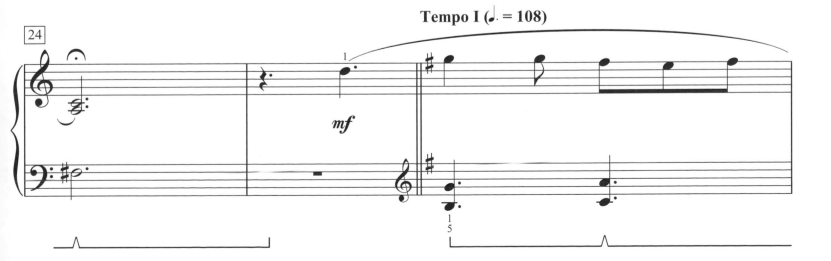

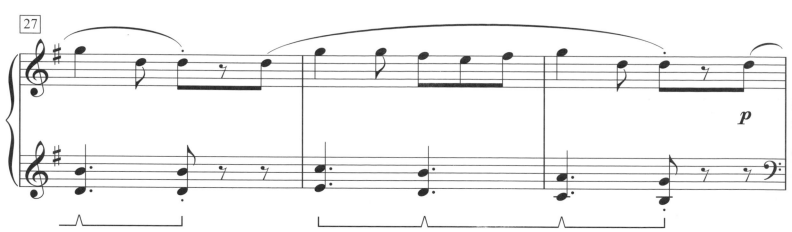

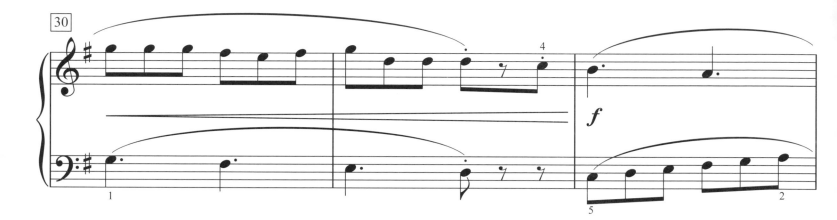

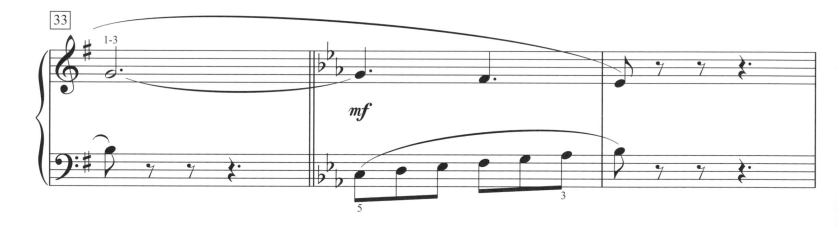

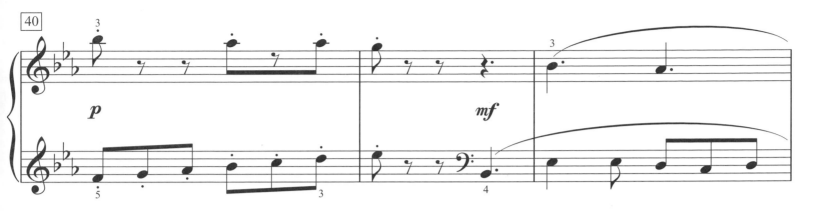

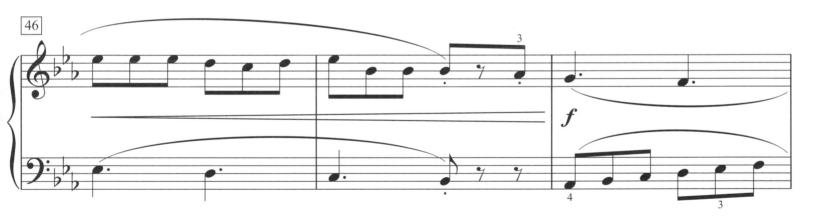

TWINKLE, TWINKLE LITTLE STAR

Traditional
Arranged by Phillip Keveren

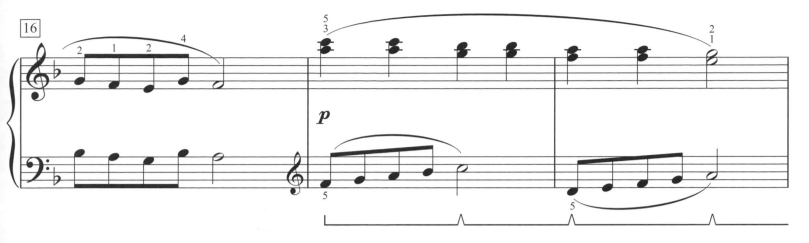

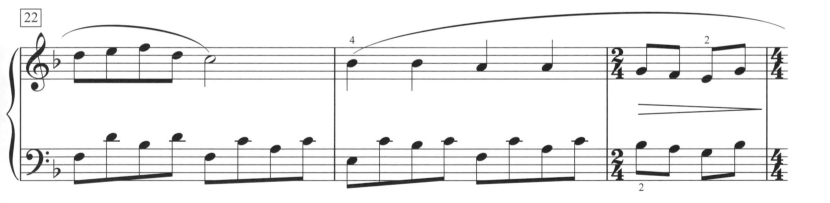

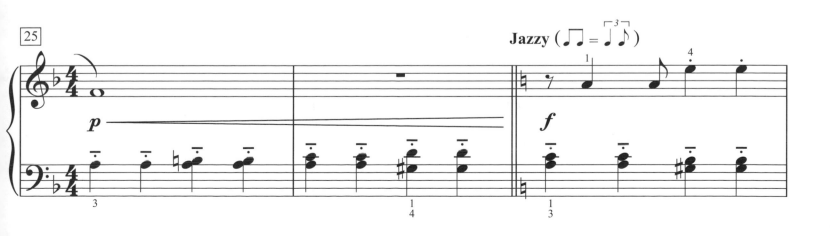

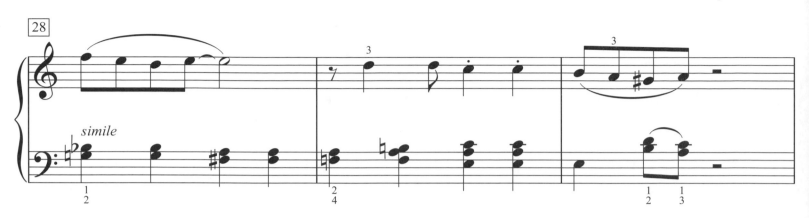

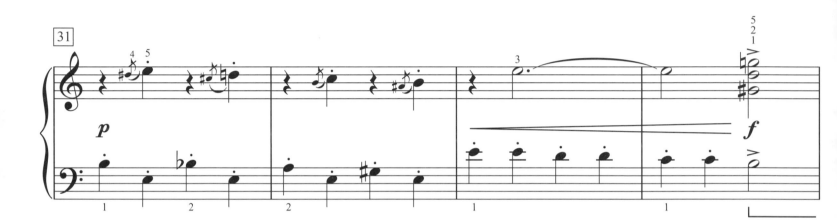

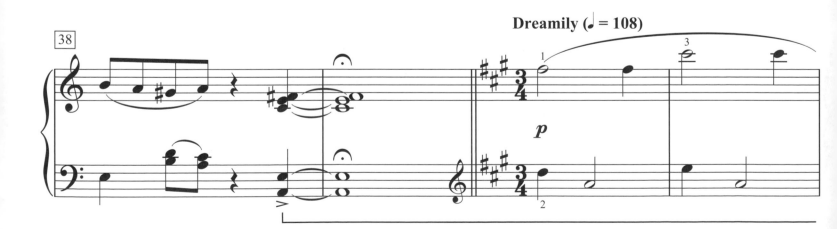

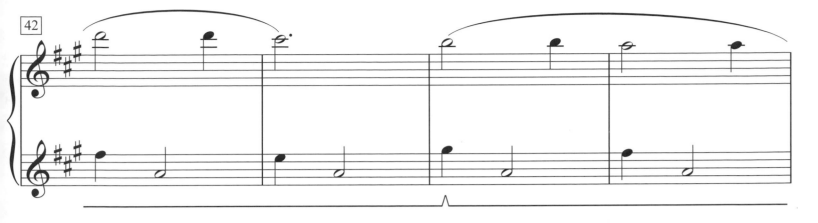

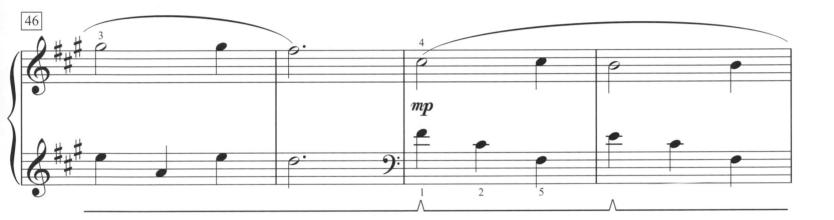

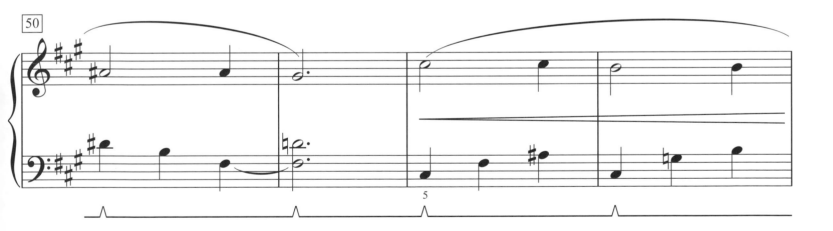

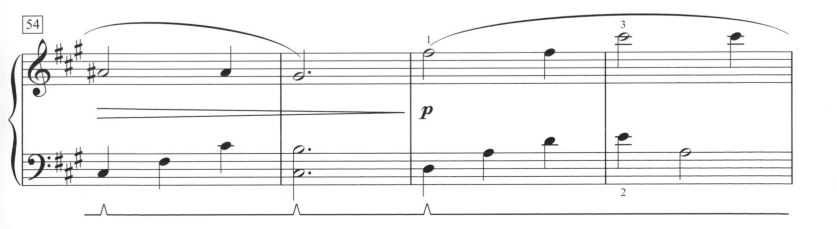

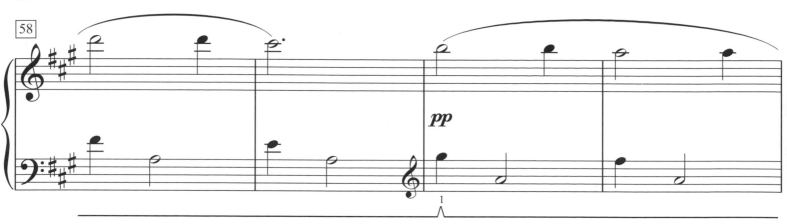

Sparkling Jig (♩. = 126)

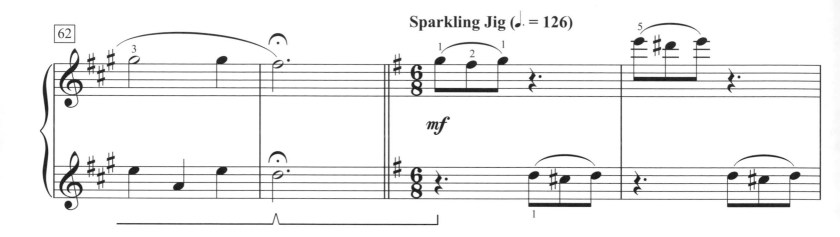

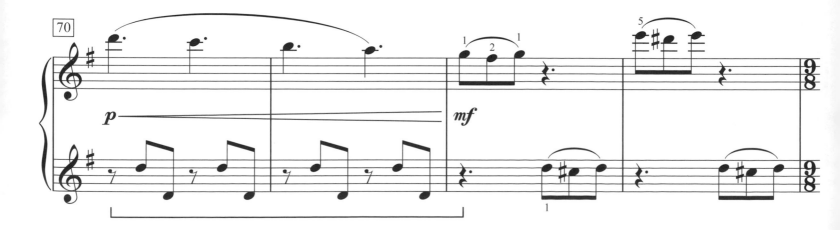

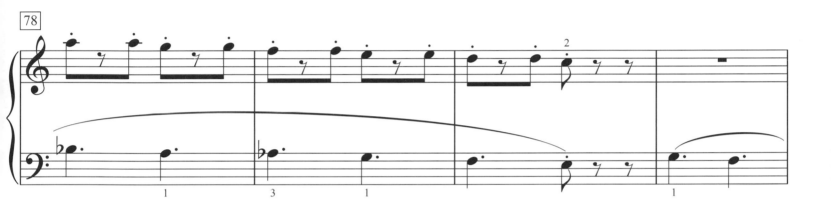

SKIP TO MY LOU

Traditional
Arranged by Phillip Keveren

March (♩ = 92)

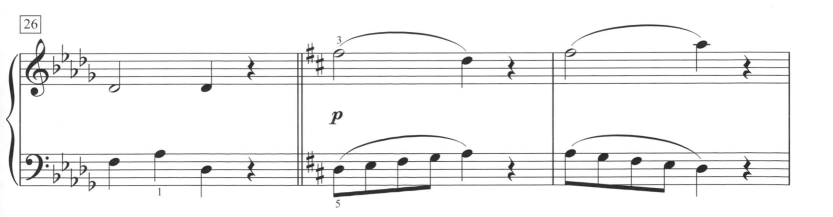